AF701007

RALPH WALDO EMERSON.

THE LITTLE BLACK BOOK

"MAY THE WISDOM OF THE GREATEST MINDS BECOME YOURS."
S. C. HOLLISTER

RENEGADE PUBLISHING

RALPH WALDO EMERSON.
THE LITTLE BLACK BOOK

Design Copyright © 2015 S.C. Hollister

Published by Renegade Publishing
California

To Ralph Waldo Emerson,
Thank you.

Contents

The Little Black Book used to be a means of getting in touch with people who could give you what you wanted; most famously understood as a Booty Call book.

But, in this 21st century version of the little black book, wisdom and knowledge are the keys to opening doors.

The design of this book invites you to meditate on the wisdom within, have focused conversations, or protect your coffee table from condensation.

May the wisdom of some of the greatest, become yours.

Ralph Waldo Emerson.

The Little Black Book

Emerson's Little Black Book

~

1. "Dare to live the life you have dreamed for yourself. Go forward and make your dreams come true."

2. "The only person you are destined to become is the person you decide to be."

3. "It is one of the blessings of old friends that you can afford to be stupid with them."

4. "What lies behind us and what lies before us are tiny matters compared to what lies within us."

5. "Always do what you are afraid to do."

6. "DO NOT GO WHERE THE PATH MAY LEAD, GO INSTEAD WHERE THERE IS NO PATH AND LEAVE A TRAIL."

7. "LIVE IN THE SUNSHINE, SWIM THE SEA, DRINK THE WILD AIR."

8. "WHAT YOU DO SPEAKS SO LOUDLY THAT I CANNOT HEAR WHAT YOU SAY."

9. "WHEN IT IS DARK ENOUGH, YOU CAN SEE THE STARS."

10. "IS IT SO BAD THEN, TO BE MISUNDERSTOOD? PYTHAGORAS WAS MISUNDERSTOOD, AND SOCRATES, AND JESUS, AND LUTHER, AND COPERNICUS, AND GALILEO, AND NEWTON, AND EVERY PURE AND WISE SPIRIT THAT EVER TOOK FLESH. TO BE GREAT IS TO BE MISUNDERSTOOD."

11. "I CANNOT REMEMBER THE BOOKS I'VE READ ANY MORE THAN THE MEALS I HAVE EATEN; EVEN SO, THEY HAVE MADE ME."

12. "ALL I HAVE SEEN TEACHES ME TO TRUST THE CREATOR FOR ALL I HAVE NOT SEEN."

13. "WHATEVER YOU DO, YOU NEED COURAGE. WHATEVER COURSE YOU DECIDE UPON, THERE IS ALWAYS SOMEONE TO TELL YOU THAT YOU ARE WRONG. THERE ARE ALWAYS DIFFICULTIES ARISING THAT TEMPT YOU TO BELIEVE YOUR CRITICS ARE RIGHT. TO MAP OUT A COURSE OF ACTION AND FOLLOW IT TO AN END REQUIRES SOME OF THE SAME COURAGE THAT A SOLDIER NEEDS. PEACE HAS VICTORIES, BUT IT TAKES BRAVE MEN AND WOMEN TO WIN THEM."

14. "The best lightning rod for your protection is your own spine."

15. "Make your own Bible. Select and collect all the words and sentences that in all your readings have been to you like the blast of a trumpet."

16. "Character is higher than intellect. A great soul will be strong to live as well as think."

17. "The happiest man is he who learns from nature the lesson of worship."

18. "God enters by a private door into every individual."

19. "Imagination is a very high sort of seeing."

20. "LOVE WHAT IS SIMPLE AND BEAUTIFUL. THESE ARE THE ESSENTIALS."

21. "LIFE IS TO BE LIVED, NOT CONTROLLED."

22. "IT IS NOT THE LENGTH OF LIFE, BUT THE DEPTH."

23. "IT IS EASY IN THE WORLD TO LIVE AFTER THE WORLD'S OPINION; IT IS EASY IN SOLITUDE TO LIVE AFTER OUR OWN; BUT THE GREAT MAN IS HE WHO IN THE MIDST OF THE CROWD KEEPS WITH PERFECT SWEETNESS THE INDEPENDENCE OF SOLITUDE."

24. "THE EARTH LAUGHS IN FLOWERS."

25. "ONCE YOU MAKE A DECISION, THE UNIVERSE CONSPIRES TO MAKE IT HAPPEN."

26. "LIFE IS A JOURNEY, NOT A DESTINATION."

27. "CULTIVATE THE HABIT OF BEING GRATEFUL FOR EVERY GOOD THING THAT COMES TO YOU, AND TO GIVE THANKS CONTINUOUSLY. AND BECAUSE ALL THINGS HAVE CONTRIBUTED TO YOUR ADVANCEMENT, YOU SHOULD INCLUDE ALL THINGS IN YOUR GRATITUDE."

28. "WITHOUT AMBITION ONE STARTS NOTHING. WITHOUT WORK ONE FINISHES NOTHING. THE PRIZE WILL NOT BE SENT TO YOU. YOU HAVE TO WIN IT."

29. "NOTHING GREAT WAS EVER ACHIEVED WITHOUT ENTHUSIASM."

30. "ADOPT THE PACE OF NATURE; HER SECRET IS PATIENCE."

31. "MAKE THE MOST OF YOURSELF... FOR THAT IS ALL THERE IS OF YOU."

32. "BE SILLY. BE HONEST. BE KIND."

33. "IF WE ENCOUNTER A MAN OF RARE INTELLECT, WE SHOULD ASK HIM WHAT BOOKS HE READS."

34. "BE NOT THE SLAVE OF YOUR OWN PAST – PLUNGE INTO THE SUBLIME SEAS, DIVE DEEP, AND SWIM FAR, SO YOU SHALL COME BACK WITH NEW SELF-RESPECT, WITH NEW POWER, AND WITH AN ADVANCED EXPERIENCE THAT SHALL EXPLAIN AND OVERLOOK THE OLD."

35. "DON'T BE TOO TIMID AND SQUEAMISH ABOUT YOUR ACTIONS. ALL LIFE IS AN EXPERIMENT. THE MORE EXPERIMENTS YOU MAKE THE BETTER."

36. YOU CANNOT DO A KINDNESS TOO SOON, FOR YOU NEVER KNOW HOW SOON IT WILL BE TOO LATE."

37. "THE ONLY WAY TO HAVE A FRIEND IS TO BE A FRIEND."

38. "A HERO IS NO BRAVER THAN AN ORDINARY MAN, BUT HE IS BRAVE FIVE MINUTES LONGER."

39. "THOUGH WE TRAVEL THE WORLD OVER TO FIND THE BEAUTIFUL, WE MUST CARRY IT WITH US, OR WE FIND IT NOT."

40. "OUR CHIEF WANT IS SOMEONE WHO WILL INSPIRE US TO BE WHAT WE KNOW WE COULD BE."

41. "SHALLOW MEN BELIEVE IN LUCK OR IN CIRCUMSTANCE. STRONG MEN BELIEVE IN CAUSE AND EFFECT."

42. "THE PURPOSE OF LIFE IS NOT TO BE HAPPY; IT IS TO BE USEFUL, TO BE HONORABLE, TO BE COMPASSIONATE, TO HAVE IT MAKE SOME DIFFERENCE THAT YOU LIVED AND LIVED WELL."

43. "A FRIEND IS A PERSON WITH WHOM I MAY BE SINCERE. BEFORE HIM I MAY THINK ALOUD. I AM ARRIVED AT LAST IN THE PRESENCE OF A MAN SO REAL AND EQUAL, THAT I MAY DROP EVEN THOSE UNDERMOST GARMENTS OF DISSIMULATION, COURTESY, AND SECOND THOUGHT, WHICH MEN NEVER PUT OFF, AND MAY DEAL WITH HIM WITH SIMPLICITY AND WHOLENESS WITH WHICH ONE CHEMICAL ATOM MEETS ANOTHER."

44. "EVERY ARTIST WAS FIRST AN AMATEUR."

45. "He is rich who owns the day, and no one owns the day who allows it to be invaded with fret and anxiety."

46. "This new day is too dear, with its hopes and invitations, to waste a moment on the yesterdays."

47. "Peace cannot be achieved through violence; it can only be attained through understanding."

48. "Guard well your spare moments. They are like uncut diamonds. Discard them and their value will never be known. Improve them and they will become the brightest gems in a useful life."

49. "PEOPLE DO NOT SEEM TO REALIZE THAT THEIR OPINION OF THE WORLD IS ALSO A CONFESSION OF THEIR CHARACTER."

50. MOST OF THE SHADOWS OF THIS LIFE ARE CAUSED BY STANDING IN ONE'S OWN SUNSHINE."

51. "WHEN FRIENDSHIPS ARE REAL, THEY ARE NOT GLASS THREADS OR FROST WORK, BUT THE SOLIDEST THINGS WE CAN KNOW."

52. "YOU BECOME WHAT YOU THINK ABOUT ALL DAY LONG."

53. "NOTHING IS AT LAST SACRED BUT THE INTEGRITY OF YOUR OWN MIND."

54. "THE MIND, ONCE STRETCHED BY A NEW IDEA, NEVER RETURNS TO ITS ORIGINAL DIMENSIONS."

55. "Envy is ignorance, imitation is suicide."

56. "Happiness is a perfume you cannot pour on others without getting some on yourself."

57. "Sometimes a scream is better than a thesis."

58. "Life is a succession of lessons which must be lived to be understood."

59. "The good news is that the moment you decide that what you know is more important than what you have been taught to believe, you will have shifted gears in your quest for abundance. Success comes from within, not from without."

60. "THE CREATION OF A THOUSAND FOREST IS IN ONE ACORN."

61. "BE YOURSELF; NO BASE IMITATOR OF ANOTHER, BUT YOUR BEST SELF. THE REI SOMETHING WHICH YOU CAN DO BETTER THAN ANOTHER. LISTEN TO THE INWARD VOICE AND BRAVELY OBEY THAT. DO THE THINGS AT WHICH YOU ARE GREAT, NOT WHAT YOU WERE NEVER MADE FOR."

62. "THERE IS CREATIVE READING AS WELL AS CREATIVE WRITING."

63. "LET ME NEVER FALL INTO THE VULGAR MISTAKE OF DREAMING THAT I AM PERSECUTED WHENEVER I AM CONTRADICTED."

64. "IN MY WALKS, EVERY MAN I MEET IS MY SUPERIOR IN SOME WAY, AND IN THAT I LEARN FROM HIM."

65. "NOTHING EXTERNAL TO YOU HAS ANY POWER OVER YOU."

66. "NATURE AND BOOKS BELONG TO THE EYES THAT SEE THEM."

67. "THERE IS A TIME IN EVERY MAN'S EDUCATION WHEN HE ARRIVES AT THE CONVICTION THAT ENVY IS IGNORANCE; THAT IMITATION IS SUICIDE; THAT HE MUST TAKE HIMSELF FOR BETTER, FOR WORSE, AS HIS PORTION; THAT THOUGH THE WIDE UNIVERSE IS FULL OF GOOD, NO KERNEL OF NOURISHING CORN CAN COME TO HIM BUT THROUGH HIS TOIL BESTOWED ON THAT PLOT OF GROUND WHICH IS GIVEN TO HIM TO TILL. THE POWER WHICH RESIDES IN HIM IS NEW IN NATURE, AND NONE BUT HE KNOWS WHAT THAT IS, WHICH HE CAN DO, NOR DOES HE KNOW UNTIL HE HAS TRIED."

68. "FEW PEOPLE KNOW HOW TO TAKE A WALK. THE QUALIFICATIONS ARE ENDURANCE, PLAIN CLOTHES, OLD SHOES, AN EYE FOR NATURE, GOOD HUMOR, VAST CURIOSITY, GOOD SPEECH, GOOD SILENCE AND NOTHING TOO MUCH."

69. "TRUST THYSELF: EVERY HEART VIBRATES TO THAT IRON STRING."

70. "THAT WHICH WE PERSIST IN DOING BECOMES EASIER TO DO. NOT THAT THE NATURE OF THE THING HAS CHANGED, BUT THAT OUR POWER TO DO HAS INCREASED."

71. "LET US BE SILENT, THAT WE MAY HEAR THE WHISPER OF GOD."

72. "THE INVARIABLE MARK OF WISDOM IS TO SEE THE MIRACULOUS IN THE COMMON."

73. "THE ORNAMENT OF A HOUSE IS THE FRIENDS WHO FREQUENT IT."

74. "IN A LIBRARY WE ARE SURROUNDED BY MANY HUNDREDS OF DEAR FRIENDS IMPRISONED BY AN ENCHANTER IN PAPER AND LEATHERN BOXES."

75. "LIFE IS SHORT, BUT THERE IS ALWAYS TIME ENOUGH FOR COURTESY."

76. "FOR EVERYTHING YOU HAVE MISSED, YOU HAVE GAINED SOMETHING ELSE, AND FOR EVERYTHING YOU GAIN, YOU LOSE SOMETHING ELSE."

77. "A FOOLISH CONSISTENCY IS THE HOBGOBLIN OF LITTLE MINDS."

78. "PEOPLE ONLY SEE WHAT THEY ARE PREPARED TO SEE."

79. "DO THE THING YOU FEAR AND THE DEATH OF FEAR IS CERTAIN."

80. "TO BE YOURSELF IN A WORLD THAT IS CONSTANTLY TRYING TO MAKE YOU SOMETHING ELSE IS THE GREATEST ACCOMPLISHMENT."

81. "FOR EVERY MINUTE YOU ARE ANGRY, YOU LOSE SIXTY SECONDS OF HAPPINESS."

82. "FINISH EACH DAY AND BE DONE WITH IT. YOU HAVE DONE WHAT YOU COULD. SOME BLUNDERS AND ABSURDITIES NO DOUBT CREPT IN; FORGET THEM AS SOON AS YOU CAN. TOMORROW IS A NEW DAY. YOU SHALL BEGIN IN SERENITY AND WITH TOO HIGH A SPIRIT TO BE ENCUMBERED WITH YOUR OLD NONSENSE."

83. "ALL MY BEST THOUGHTS WERE STOLEN BY THE ANCIENTS."

84. "NOTHING CAN BRING YOU PEACE BUT YOURSELF."

85. "COMMON SENSE IS GENIUS DRESSED IN ITS WORKING CLOTHES."

86. "LOVE AND YOU SHALL BE LOVED."

87. "SORROW LOOKS BACK. WORRY LOOKS AROUND. FAITH LOOKS UP."

88. "WE ARE ALWAYS READY TO LIVE BUT NEVER LIVING."

89. "NONE OF US WILL EVER ACCOMPLISH ANYTHING EXCELLENT OR COMMANDING EXCEPT WHEN HE LISTENS TO THIS WHISPER WHICH IS HEARD BY HIM ALONE."

90. "INSIST ON YOURSELF; NEVER IMITATE. YOUR OWN GIFT YOU CAN OFFER WITH THE CUMULATIVE FORCE OF A WHOLE LIFE'S CULTIVATION, BUT OF THE ADOPTED TALENT OF ANOTHER, YOU HAVE ONLY AN EXTEMPORANEOUS, HALF POSSESSION."

91. "FRIENDSHIP, LIKE THE IMMORTALITY OF THE SOUL, IS TOO GOOD TO BE BELIEVED. WHEN FRIENDSHIP IS REAL, THEY ARE NOT GLASS THREADS OR FROST WORK BUT THE SOLIDEST THINGS WE KNOW."

92. "FEAR ALWAYS SPRINGS FROM IGNORANCE."

93. "EVEN IN THE MUD AND SCUM OF THINGS, SOMETHING ALWAYS, ALWAYS SINGS."

94. "THE YEARS TEACH MUCH THE DAYS NEVER KNOW."

95. "YOU HAVE JUST DINED, AND HOWEVER SCRUPULOUSLY THE SLAUGHTERHOUSE IS CONCEALED IN THE GRACEFUL DISTANCE OF MILES, THERE IS COMPLICITY."

96. "BE GOOD TO YOUR WORK, YOUR WORD, AND YOUR FRIEND."

97. "WHEN YOU WERE BORN YOU WERE CRYING AND EVERYONE ELSE WAS SMILING. LIVE YOUR LIFE SO AT THE END, YOU'RE THE ONE WHO IS SMILING AND EVERYONE ELSE IS CRYING."

98. "A CHILD IS A CURLY, DIMPLED LUNATIC."

99. "NOTHING CAN BRING YOU PEACE BUT YOURSELF."

100. "THE SECRET OF EDUCATION LIES IN RESPECTING THE PUPIL. IT IS NOT FOR YOU TO CHOOSE WHAT HE SHALL KNOW, WHAT HE SHALL DO. IT IS CHOSEN AND FOREORDAINED AND HE ONLY HOLDS THE KEY TO HIS OWN SECRET."

101. "THE WISE MAN IN THE STORM PRAYS TO GOD NOT FOR SAFETY FROM DANGER, BUT FOR DELIVERANCE FROM FEAR."

102. "IN THE HIGHEST CIVILIZATION, THE BOOK IS STILL THE HIGHEST DELIGHT. HE WHO HAS ONCE KNOWN ITS SATISFACTIONS IS PROVIDED WITH A RESOURCE AGAINST CALAMITY."

103. "BAD TIMES HAVE A SCIENTIFIC VALUE. THESE ARE OCCASIONS A GOOD LEARNER WOULD NOT MISS."

104. "WHAT I MUST DO IS ALL THAT CONCERNS ME, NOT WHAT PEOPLE THINK. THIS RULE, EQUALLY ARDUOUS IN ACTUAL AND INTELLECTUAL LIFE, MAY SERVE FOR THE WHOLE DISTINCTION BETWEEN GREATNESS AND MEANNESS. IT IS THE HARDER, BECAUSE YOU WILL ALWAYS FIND THOSE WHO THINK THEY KNOW WHAT IS YOUR DUTY BETTER THAN YOU KNOW IT. IT IS EASY IN THE WORLD TO LIVE AFTER THE WORLD'S OPINION; IT IS EASY IN SOLITUDE TO LIVE AFTER OUR OWN; BUT THE GREAT MAN IS HE WHO IN THE MIDST OF THE CROWD KEEPS WITH PERFECT SWEETNESS THE INDEPENDENCE OF SOLITUDE."

105. "WHAT IS A WEED? A PLANT WHOSE VIRTUES HAVE NOT YET BEEN DISCOVERED."

106. "FOR EACH NEW MORNING WITH ITS LIGHT, FOR REST AND SHELTER OF THE NIGHT, FOR HEALTH AND FOOD, FOR LOVE AND FRIENDS, FOR EVERYTHING THY GOODNESS SENDS."

107. "IF THE STARS SHOULD APPEAR BUT ONE NIGHT EVERY THOUSAND YEARS, HOW MAN WOULD MARVEL AND ADORE."

108. "EVERY WALL IS A DOOR."

109. "WHOSO WOULD BE A MAN MUST BE A NONCONFORMIST."

110. "WE ACQUIRE THE STRENGTH WE HAVE OVERCOME."

111. "THERE IS ONE REASON FOR DRESSING WELL, NAMELY THAT DOGS RESPECT IT, AND WILL NOT ATTACK YOU IN GOOD CLOTHES."

112. "TOMORROW IS A NEW DAY; BEGIN IT WELL AND SERENELY AND WITH TOO HIGH A SPIRIT TO BE ENCUMBERED WITH YOUR OLD NONSENSE."

113. "LIFE CONSISTS OF WHAT MAN IS THINKING ABOUT ALL DAY."

114. "BEWARE WHAT YOU SET YOUR HEART UPON. FOR IT SURELY SHALL BE YOURS."

115. "IT IS ONE OF THE BEAUTIFUL COMPENSATIONS OF LIFE THAT NO MAN CAN SINCERELY TRY TO HELP ANOTHER WITHOUT HELPING HIMSELF."

116. "TRUST INSTINCT TO THE END, EVEN THOUGH YOU CAN GIVE NO REASON."

117. "SCATTER JOY!"

118. "Don't be pushed by your problems; be led by your dreams."

119. "Fiction reveals truth that reality obscures."

120. Enthusiasm is one of the most powerful engines of success. When you do a thing, do it with all your might. Put your whole soul into it. Stamp it with your own personality. Be active, be energetic, be enthusiastic and faithful, and you will accomplish your object. Nothing great was ever achieved without enthusiasm."

121. "Whatever games are played with us, we must play no games with ourselves, but deal in our privacy with the last honesty and truth."

122. LIFE IS A TRAIN OF MOODS LIKE A STRING OF BEADS; AND AS WE PASS THROUGH THEM THEY PROVE TO BE MANY COLORED LENSES, WHICH PAINT THE WORLD THEIR OWN HUE, AND EACH SHOWS U ONLY WHAT LIES IN ITS OWN FOCUS."

123. "THE SECRET OF EDUCATION LIES IN RESPECTING THE PUPIL."

124. "INSIST ON YOURSELF; NEVER IMITATE. YOUR OWN GIFT YOU CAN PRESENT EVERY MOMENT WITH THE CUMULATIVE FORCE OF A WHOLE LIFE'S CULTIVATION; BUT OF THE ADOPTED TALENT OF ANOTHER YOU HAVE ONLY AN EXTEMPORANEOUS HALF POSSESSION. THAT WHICH EACH CAN DO BEST, NONE BUT HIS MAKER CAN TEACH HIM."

125. "MANY EYES GO THROUGH THE MEADOW, BUT FEW SEE THE FLOWERS IN IT."

126. "FEAR DEFEATS MORE PEOPLE THAN ANY OTHER ONE THING IN THE WORLD."

127. "MY LIFE IS NOT AN APOLOGY, BUT A LIFE. IT IS FOR ITSELF AND NOT FOR A SPECTACLE. I MUCH PREFER THAT IT SHOULD BE OF A LOWER STRAIN, SO IT BE GENUINE AND EQUAL, THAN THAT IT SHOULD BE GLITTERING AND UNSTEADY."

128. "THE ANCESTOR OF EVERY ACTION IS A THOUGHT."

129. "IF I HAVE LOST CONFIDENCE IN MYSELF, I HAVE THE UNIVERSE AGAINST ME."

130. "IT IS HAPPY TALENT TO KNOW HOW TO PLAY."

131. "TO LAUGH OFTEN AND MUCH; TO WIN THE RESPECT OF INTELLIGENT PEOPLE AND THE AFFECTION OF CHILDREN, TO LEAVE THE WORLD A BETTER PLACE, TO KNOW EVEN ONE LIFE HAS BREATHED EASIER BECAUSE YOU HAVE LIVED, THIS IS TO HAVE SUCCEEDED."

132. "IN ORDER FOR ONE TO LEARN THE IMPORTANT LESSONS OF LIFE, ONE MUST FIRST OVERCOME A FEAR EACH DAY."

133. "SPEAK WHAT YOU THINK TODAY IN HARD WORDS AND TOMORROW SPEAK WHAT TOMORROW THINKS IN HARD WORDS AGAIN, THOUGHT IT CONTRADICT EVERYTHING YOU SAID TODAY."

134. "THE WORLD MAKES WAY FOR THE MAN WHO KNOWS WHERE HE IS GOING."

135. "COLLEGES HATE GENIUSES, JUST AS CONVENTS HATE SAINTS."

136. "THE REWARD OF A THING WELL DONE IS HAVING DONE IT."

137. "ONE OF THE ILLUSIONS OF LIFE IS THAT THE PRESENT HOUR IS NOT THE CRITICAL, DECISIVE HOUR. WRITE IT ON YOUR HEART THAT EVERY DAY IS THE BEST DAY OF THE YEAR."

138. "THE RELIGION OF ONE AGE IS THE LITERARY ENTERTAINMENT OF THE NEXT."

139. "THE ARTIST ALWAYS HAS THE MASTER IN HIS EYES."

140. "DON'T WASTE YOURSELF IN REJECTION, NOR BARK AGAINST THE BAD, BUT CHANT THE BEAUTY OF THE GOOD."

141. "SOW A THOUGHT AND YOU REAP AN ACTION; SOW AN ACT AND YOU REAP A HABIT; SOW A HABIT AND YOU REAP A CHARACTER; SOW A CHARACTER AND YOU REAP A DESTINY."

142. "THE WORLD BELONGS TO THE ENERGETIC."

...

More Titles in *The Little Black Book* series:

- Alaska Noon
- Albert Einstein
- Benjamin Franklin
- Bill Gates
- Bruce Lee
- Buddha
- Elon Musk
- Helen Keller
- Ida B. Wells
- Jesus Christ
- Johnny Depp
- Mahatma Gandhi
- Martin Luther King Junior
- Mark Zuckerberg
- Nicholas Cage
- Nikola Tesla
- Oprah Winfrey
- Richard Branson
- Russell Brand
- Steve Jobs
- Walt Disney

If there is someone you'd like to see added to *The Little Black Book* series, please leave a comment in this books review section on Amazon.com.

31682260R00026

Made in the USA
Middletown, DE
02 January 2019